C000219356

Oxted

in old picture postcards volume 1

Roger Packham

European Library ZALTBOMMEL / THE NETHERLANDS

GB ISBN 90 288 3493 1

© 1987 European Library – Zaltbommel/The Netherlands
Fourth edition, 2000: reprint of the original edition of 1987.

European Library
post office box 49
NL – 5300 AA Zaltbommel/The Netherlands
telephone: 0031 418 513144
fax: 0031 418 515515
e-mail:publisher@eurobib.nl

INTRODUCTION

The magnificent High Street of old Oxted was for centuries part of the well-travelled west-east route through Surrey, a few miles from the Kent boundary and Westerham. Well-blessed with inns and a variety of outstanding domestic buildings, the old High Street remains as a noble testimony to the splendid architecture of the Tudor period and earlier, despite a few sad losses sustained in the last war.

This book is not a history of Oxted, although it is hoped that the notes will be enlightening. It should be observed, though, that the village of Oxted – Acstede in Domesday Book – is an established Saxon settlement and that the parish church and local mills are mentioned in that massive compilation: both Domesday Book and St. Mary's Church celebrate novocentenaries in 1986.

It is one of Oxted's mysteries that St. Mary's is such a distance from the old village but W.F. Mumford in 1949 explained it thus: 'Widely separated from the village by fields and the marshy waste that is now Master Park, was the Church whose site had in early Christian times been determined by the existing pagan burial ground.' It would be interesting to know if *there* is any evidence of pre-Christian burials and why the church's situation in relation to the village is so different to the established pattern of Saxon settlements.

The population of the village would have been in the low hundreds for centuries and it is only in modern times that numbers have increased significantly. The influence of the railway which arrived in 1884 cannot be overestimated. Oxted Station is a considerable distance from the old village but an entirely new settlement arose around Station Road East and Station Road West and many well-planned roads were constructed. New Oxted, as this area was known at the beginning of the present century, quickly gained its own identity and the railway provided great impetus to local industries and has made commuting possible for the last hundred years.

Much more recently the old village has become something of a backwater to passing traffic, firstly by the construction of the Oxted by-pass (A25) and now, within the last few years, of the M25. Though the effects of the motorway cutting through Green Belt land, south of the North Downs, are to be deplored, it is a reassuring fact that those splendid High Street buildings enjoy far less disruption and the prospect of ultimate structural damage is much diminished.

The postcards used in this book were published in the early years of this century when a lively commercial enterprise led to an absorbing photographic record being compiled, especially in the decade before the Great War. Postcard companies produced cards for local traders such as Lock, Cox, Johnson, Gregory, Richardson and Webster in competition with outside publishers who introduced their own views e.g. Frith, Valentine, W.H. Smith, Homewood, W.A. Field, Gordon Smith and Ace. Additionally, local photographers such as C.L. King and W. Suter produced good quality cards which all add to the comprehensive record. In this Golden Age of postcards, everyone sent them; they were eagerly awaited by the recipients and they were widely collected. It has proved a fascinating exercise to a modern collector to re-construct the Oxted of the early years of the twentieth century.

I have started the book with a tour up and down the old High Street, taking in a glimpse of Brook Hill. This is followed by a visit to St. Mary's Church and the Master Park area. Before moving to New Oxted, the local mill and lime kilns are included to show the industrial acitivity of the area. The central section is devoted to Station Road West and Station Road East and some adjoining developments are also featured. A few stately houses then follow before we take a look at the Oxted districts to the south – Barrow Green, Hurst Green, Holland and Merle Common. The Oxted Prize Band brings up the rear.

I warmly recommend 'Oxted Explored' by Annette Wells and Kay Percy (Tandridge District Council, 1975) for those interested in the architectural legacy of old Oxted and readily acknowledge information which I have used for notes. However, there is a definite need for a full history of this outstanding Surrey locality and it is hoped that the present work will appeal to all residents and those familiar with Oxted in the way it re-creates the atmosphere of the gentle era before the onslaught of the motor car.

September 1986   Roger Packham
                                                        Caterham

OLD OXTED.

1. A view of the old High Street, looking east about 1905, shows the old sign for The Bell Inn prominently displayed. On the main west-east route to Kent (A25) for many years, the High Street is now by-passed to its great advantage. This postcard was published by W.A. Field of South Norwood in his Surrey Series (No. 417).

High Street. Oxted.

Cox's Series. 1058.

2. Two boys stand and watch the photographer in this charming view of the High Street, looking west, taken about 1910. The tiles have been removed from the upper storey of The Bell and the inn sign has become less noticeable. Beyond the inn, the Old Dairy advertises R. White's ginger beer, soda and milk. Beadles Cottage and the White House stand proudly beyond the cross roads.

3. This is an earlier photograph of the cross roads by The Bell by A.H. Homewood of Burgess Hill, about 1905 with Beadles Lane to the left and Brook Hill to the right, beyond the inn sign. A delivery horse and cart proceeds at a leisurely pace, followed by a respectably dressed couple untroubled by the traffic nuisance of later years.

4. Four Edwardian girls stand at the entrance to Brook Hill in this Francis Frith postcard, which was published in 1908. Lenton's Model Dairy (left) advertises teas: the solid building dates from about 1400 with a modern shop front. Today it is the office of a chartered architect.

High Street, Oxted, Surrey.

5. A.H. Homewood of Burgess Hill published this postcard of the High Street, looking east, which was posted in July, 1907. The sign boards of The George and The Crown can be seen overlooking the road. In 1904, T. Troughton's London Stores advertised china, glass, ironmongery and bedding in addition to being a grocer, draper and wine, spirit and beer merchant.

6. This is a later view of the High Street, in Cox's Photo Series, and was posted in September 1911. Three girls stand outside Kenton's furniture shop and a group of boys in the centre of the photograph also appear to be aware of the camera. The wine merchants on the right exists today as Unwins.

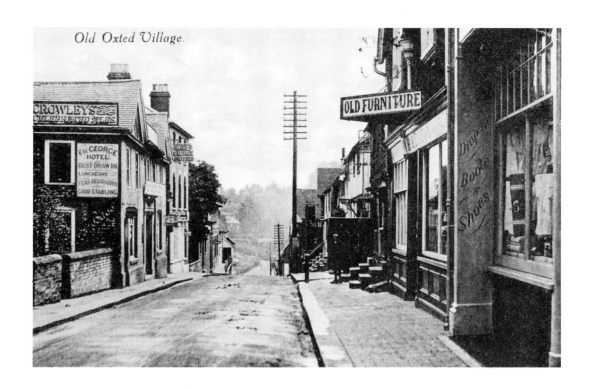

Old Oxted Village.

7. This R.T.M. Series postcard was posted in 1920 and shows some bold advertising on The George Hotel. Crowley's ales were brewed in Croydon and Bass, from Burton-on-Trent, was also available. The wing on the east of The George appears to have been built in the fifteenth century. In later years The George sold beers from Page & Overton, another Croydon brewery.

High Street, Oxted.

Cox's Series

8. Moving further down the High Street, this photograph of about 1911 shows the attractive houses on the right leading down to The Crown. They rejoice in the names of Catmint, Old Town House, Flaxman Cottages and The Nest. The first two are part of a sixteenth century hall house.

High Street, Oxted. Looking West.

9. An A.H. Homewood postcard, posted in 1906, shows The Crown Inn and the High Street looking east (not west as shown). The inn was known as The Crown and Anchor when William Roberts was the innkeeper in 1826. The main building dates from the eighteenth century although the frontage was added about 1870.

10. Oxted High Street is pictured about 1930 in the Golden Series and The Crown Inn has become The Crown Hotel selling Westerham ales. Opposite The Crown stands a quaint milk cart advertising pure, rich milk and further down the hill, a brewery lorry is delivering some barrels to The Wheatsheaf.

11. This postcard was published by A. Stripe of Oxted, about 1912 and shows the High Street, looking east, below The Crown Inn. The pinafored girls have no fears from the horse-drawn vehicles and the wheelbarrows in the bottom right-hand corner indicate that some building work was being undertaken at The Crown. The shops on the left of the picture are now private houses – The Old Post Office, Fraser's Cottage and Saddlers.

12. A drayman and his faithful horse pose for a photographer outside The Wheatsheaf at the bottom of the High Street on a summer's day about 1910. The inn appears to stand on the site of the mill shown on maps of 1729 and 1760 and it has a slate-roofed wing at the rear which is much earlier in character than the building shown above.

West Hill, Oxted.

13. At the foot of the High Street, the main road continues eastwards towards Limpsfield and the Kentish boundary. The road to the left leads towards the new part of Oxted which has grown up around the railway station. The charming house in the triangle has been replaced by Langley House. This J.B. Lock postcard was published about 1911.

14. A postcard in Cox's Photo Series, posted in New Oxted in 1916, starts our return up the High Street. The bridge over the river may be seen before The Wheatsheaf and the whole street is remarkably free from any traffic. The house on the left is Riverside.

15. This is W. Suter's view of the High Street, looking west and very much en fête presumably for the Jubilee of 1935 or for the Coronation of 1937. Several of the buildings on the right-hand side were destroyed by enemy action. The notice board (right) is owned by the 4th Battalion Queens Royal Company-Oxted Division.

S.5243.   HIGH STREET OXTED.

16. A Kingsway Series postcard records the High Street shortly before the Great War. Beyond The Wheatsheaf are a coachbuilder and a fishmonger and the Oxted children show their fascination for the photographer. The building housing the coachbuilder has been replaced by a modern featureless residence.

CROWN HILL, OXTED.

17. This is another view of the High Street looking west and was published by W.A. Field (Surrey Series No. 416). Note that The Wheatsheaf has not yet had the modern decorative timbering added to its exterior. Bushell, Watkins & Smith Ltd. was formed by the merger of two Westerham and a Sevenoaks brewery (A. Smith) in 1899. The date of the photograph is about 1905.

18. Walter Cox, stationer and newsagent, Post Office, Oxted published this postcard which was posted in New Oxted in 1917. Several soldiers walk down the High Street and an early motor car starts its climb: the hill was macadamised about 1924-25 when the gradient was improved.

S 17829 High Street, Old Oxted

19. H. Spillett's coach building business has moved up the hill to the premises which were earlier occupied by the fishmonger (see No. 16). A motor cycle, motor car and lorry give a small indication of the transport revolution to follow in this Kingsway postcard which was posted from Twickenham in 1929. Note Stone Cottage on the extreme right of the picture.

20. This pre-First World War postcard shows the High Street looking west from outside The George. Kenton's furniture shop may be seen on the left and towards the centre of the photo, beyond the cross roads, is The White House which dates from about 1760.

Sandy Lane & "Bell Inn", Old Oxted.

21. This 1920s view was taken at the cross roads looking north towards Brook Hill and Sandy Lane. The Bell Inn appears to have been built about 1500 and was recorded as The Five Bells in 1805. The building on the left is the Old Dairy.

22. This is an Edwardian view of Brook Hill in Field's Surrey Series (No. 419). The two outside stone steps are shown in John Hassell's painting of 1825. The tiles on the upper storey of the house to the extreme right were replaced by plaster about 1910 when it was decided to display more of The Bell's original timbers.

23. Further down Brook Hill four children pose for a photographer about 1912. The houses on the left would have only been built in the preceding years and are now obscured by the concrete pillars which carry the A25 traffic along the Oxted by-pass.

St. Mary's Church, Oxted.

J.B. Lock's
Real Photo Series.

24. J.B. Lock's postcard of St. Mary's Church shows the massive strength of the tower about 1912. The Church has, in 1986, been vigorously celebrating its novocentenary with a busy programme of activities.

S 5245   OXTED CHURCH.

25. A Kingsway postcard of about 1912 shows St. Mary's and its burial grounds looking west. Note the churchyard cross to the left of the picture. In the seventeenth century Aubrey, writing of Oxted, referred to the 'church with a handsome spire' but in July 1719 a terrible thunderstorm broke over Oxted and the spire was struck by lightning and destroyed.

26. St. Mary's Parish Church is pictured by S. & W. looking from Court Farm in a postcard, dated August 1912. The farm has now disappeared and has been replaced by some modern homes on the south side of the church. The wagon on the right hand side of the picture belonged to Berry & Sons, corn, coal and flour merchants from Oxted, Limpsfield and Caterham.

27. The churchyard cross is pictured about 1912 looking north towards the North Downs and the railway embankment. The inscription reads: *In memory of all who rest in this churchyard and of Katherine Emily Hoskins, eldest daughter of Charles Hoskins Master of Barrow Green, Oxted and for 22 years wife of Major E.B. Bengough. She died on 27th June 1908 aged 62 years. The souls of the righteous are in the hand of God.*

The Churchyard Cross, Oxted.

Oxted Cricket Ground.

Gregory's Oxted Series.

28. The sight screens of Oxted Cricket Ground are pictured here on a postcard published by Gregory's Oxted Series which was posted in July 1909. Note St. Mary's Church and the North Downs to the left of the picture. The present Oxted Cricket Club takes its formation date as 1891 although there is a record of Oxted playing Sundridge in 1855.

29. Three horses pull an interesting agricultural implement along the road outside Oxted Recreation Ground in another postcard by Gregory's about 1909. Cows graze peacefully in front of the church beyond which can be seen the Oxted Chalk Pit. The wooden fence was just below The Hoskins Arms and can be seen in No. 41.

J.B. Lock's.
Real Photo Series.

View of the North Downs, Oxted.   6678.

30. J.B. Lock's postcard shows a lady by the entrance to the Oxted Recreation Ground with a rather uncomfortable looking pushchair. The cricket square appears to be fenced off and the hedge shown in the previous photograph has been replaced by railings and a fence. The date is about 1914.

View of the North Downs, Oxted.

30665

J.B. Lock's
Real Photo Series.

31. Another J.B. Lock postcard about 1912 shows a leafy Church Lane looking north from the Hoskins Arms. Today the War Memorial would be visible by the gate and modern flats and Master Close would dominate the right hand side of Church Lane.

Oxted Mill.

10947. J. B. Lock's Copyright Series, Oxted

32. Posted in July 1908, this J.B. Lock postcard shows the fine buildings of Oxted Mill, probably on the same site as one of the mills recorded in Domesday Book. The older part is the two storey building with the projecting lucomb. The undershot wheel once turned outside the end of the older mill but was covered in when additions were made in 1893 when it was made to work alongside the water turbine by which the machinery in the new (three storey) mill is powered.

The Mill Stream, Oxted.

Cox's Photo Series

33. This postcard in Cox's Photo Series was posted in June 1922 and is a reminder of the number of streams which rise in the North Downs above Oxted and provide the infant strength to the mighty River Medway driving both Oxted Mill and, a little farther downstream, Coltsford Mill. The rubbish shown in the bottom right-hand corner of the photo proves that litter is not entirely a modern nuisance.

34. The Lime Kilns at Oxted are pictured by J.B. Lock in a postcard posted in 1915 showing the chalk incursions into the North Downs, which is a common industrial feature in Surrey with ancient origins. The opening of the railway at Oxted in 1884 provided a far reaching market for the local lime.

35. The celebrated photographer W.H. Drake of Thornton Heath has climbed to the top of the North Downs for this 1920s view of Oxted Chalk Pits. The lime kilns may be seen on the right of the centre and the road on the left is Chalk Pit Lane. The single storey building on the left is believed to be The Oxted Chalk Pit public house whose licensee in 1892 was Thomas Wales.

36. An elegantly dressed lady awaits a train at Oxted and Limpsfield Station about 1914. Three members of the railway staff are conscious of the camera on the down side platform and their hand-carts are in evidence on both platforms. The line opened as the Croydon, Oxted & East Grinstead Railway in 1884 and apart from passengers, conducted a busy trade in coal, lime and (from Lingfield) bricks and race horses.

S 5246   OXTED STATION.

37. A Kingsway card of about 1912 shows a busy up side platform with a well-stocked bookstall. The station has remained largely unaltered for today's commuter passengers but the coal and delivery sidings on the up side were removed in 1969.

Caxton House, Oxted

Valentines Series

38. This postcard shows Caxton House on the right and the Hoskins Arms hotel on the left and was posted in Limpsfield exactly eighty years ago. Two small girls stand in front of J.B. Lock's printing and stationery shop which, in 1904, also advertised fancy goods and toys; post card albums; photo albums and frames; bookbinding and an agency for art pottery and dyeing and cleaning. Twenty local views in a book could be bought for a shilling (five pence).

Hoskins Arms Hotel, Oxted.

109472 J. B. Lock's Copyright Series, Oxted.

39. The Hoskins Arms hotel is pictured in Edwardian times by J.B. Lock and St. Mary's Church may be seen to the left. In 1892 the owner was Charles Hoskins Master and the licensee was Thomas Tucker serving railway travellers and others. Twelve years later it offered stabling, a concert and banqueting hall, coffee, dining and billiard rooms, tennis courts and bowling green as well as hiring of horses and carriages and petrol.

Station Parade.
Oxted.

40. A fine view in the Golden Series posted in 1933, shows the mature oak tree and seat in front of Caxton House. Looking towards the station in the distance can be seen the Hoskins Arms and the Plaza Cinema on the left. The latter was built about 1930 by C.A. Williams and has some splendid mock Tudor features. The lorry on the right advertises Castrol – an omen for the advent of the motor car for the masses.

S 5247   **STATION ROAD WEST. OXTED.**

41. A postman and a railway worker (on bicycle) approach the camera in this Kingsway post-card published before the Great War. The neat hedge on the left leads to the Hoskins Arms and the mock Tudor shops of Caxton House on the right display their wares on a dusty summer's day.

Station Road West, Oxted.

J.B.Lock's
"Real Photo" Series.

42. J.B. Lock's postcard which was posted at New Oxted in April 1913 shows the busy Station Road West leading to the station. Two gentlemen pass the time of day by the signpost beneath the leafless oak tree. They may be discussing the early motor car or perhaps admiring Caxton House, built by John Williams in the early 1900s.

The Old Surrey Hounds   *Copyright C. L. King Oxted.*

43. C.L. King has captured the meet of the Old Surrey Hounds in a lively postcard which was posted in 1912. In 1910, Major C.G.C. Leveson-Gower began his famous Mastership of the Old Surrey Hounds which, in 1915, amalgamated with the Burstow Hunt to form the Old Surrey and Burstow Foxhounds. C.L. King was advertised in 1904 as being a landscape and general photographer of 1 Station Road, New Oxted.

STATION ROAD WEST, OXTED   1820

44. A pre-First World War postcard shows Station Road West, looking away from the station towards the signpost and the oak tree (right of centre). W. Wood's dairy is now The Good Food Shop and the left hand turn beyond is Hoskins Road.

New Oxted, Station Road West & P. O.

45. Oxted Station can be seen here from Station Road West in a postcard published by Frith of Reigate in 1908. The estate agency on the left hand side is in the name of Seale, Swan & Seale. Lloyds Bank now occupies the double gabled building on the left and today's Post Office is sited out of the picture to the left. The gable on the right still has an inscription: Oxted Corn Stores Berry and Sons.

Station Road East, New Oxted.

Johnson's Series. 1175.

46. This postcard in the Johnson's Series shows Station Road East as it appeared just before the First World War. The premises of H.H. Blades are now occupied by Walker's Textiles but the company still exists a short distance away in Amy Road, the left hand turning, above.

Station Road, Oxted, Surrey.

47. This Edwardian postcard, published by A.H. Homewood of Burgess Hill, again shows the ironmonger's premises on the left, where Challenge Motor Oil may be obtained. St. Michael's in the middle distance is today largely obscured by trees. Gregory's tobacconist shop on the right has a good selection of local view postcards. The shop is now that of Ibbett Mosely, the estate agents.

Station Road East, Oxted.

,09464   J B Lock's Copyright Series, Oxted

48. J.B. Lock published this view of Station Road East on a postcard posted in March, 1907. Only two trees remain today on the left and the neat fences on the right have disappeared with the conversion of the houses into shop premises. Shops have also been added lower down on the left.

Station Approach, New Oxted.

49. This early 1930s view of Station Road East shows the growing popularity of the motor car. Blades' ironmongery shop continues to display its wares on the left hand side and three shops down on the right can be seen Johnson's confectionery and tobacconist shop. The pillar box is today sited on the opposite side of the road.

New Oxted, Station Approach, East.

50. The station building on the down side may be seen left of centre in this Frith postcard which was published in 1908. Looking westwards, this is still a familiar approach today but the large house on the right has given way to a modern shoe shop and only the furthest of the single storey shops survives.

Station Road, [looking South] Oxted, Surrey.

51. This postcard by A.H. Homewood was posted from Westerham in 1908 and shows Station Road looking towards Gregory's tobacconist shop in the centre of the picture and the right-hand turn towards the station. The house on the left is now occupied by Publex International, on the corner of Beatrice Road but the houses and non-conformist church opposite have been demolished in favour of Tandridge Motor Centre, Budgens and Freeman, Hardy & Willis.

Station Road, (looking North) Oxted, Surrey.

52. Another Homewood postcard shows Station Road from the left hand entrance to the station looking towards the North Downs. All the houses on the left of the picture have been replaced by shops but those on the right still survive. The twin gabled shops are now occupied by House of Lloyd and Pet Fayre and Messrs. Sainsbury's shop would be on the extreme right by Amy Road. The card was posted in 1908.

Station Road, Oxted.

53. This postcard, published by A.H. Homewood, was posted in 1906 and shows some fine houses on the east side of Station Road, now known as Snatts Hill. The horse's load looks formidable on a warm summer's day and this is another scene overlooked by the North Downs.

54. This Edwardian view of Station Road East, published by Gregory, was posted in 1909. A nanny pushes a pram up the hill past a handsome delivery horse and cart. Note the gas holder to the left of the centre. All the houses on the right hand side are easily recognisable today but the road is called Snatts Hill.

East Hill Road, Oxted.

2167

Y.B. Locks.
Real Photo Series.

55. East Hill Road is photographed from near Caxton House on this Lock postcard of about 1912. Today the Police Station would be just out of view on the right hand side and local traffic climbs the hill towards the Westerham Road (A25).

Blue House Road, Oxted.

56. Three Edwardian gentlemen with walking sticks take a summer stroll along Blue House Road in a Homewood postcard, posted in Brighton in 1907. Oxted Grammar School (1929) and The Barn Theatre (1924) have been subsequent additions to a still pleasant road. The house on the right is Hamelin House (No. 116) at the Limpsfield end of the road.

Woodhurst Park, Oxted.

Gregory's
PhotoSeries.

57. The opening of the railway line led inevitably to the development of the Oxted locality and this photograph by Gregory's shows some fine houses built amongst some mature woodland. The date would be around 1912. The Card House and Hoders are two listed buildings in Woodhurst Park.

The Viaduct from Woodhurst Lane, Oxted.

Gregory's Oxted Series.

58. This Gregory postcard shows the railway viaduct from Woodhurst Lane about 1912, looking north. The sturdy brick pillars have supported the railway for over a hundred years, a tribute to the engineering skills of the Victorians. Woodhurst Lane now has a row of modern, desirable residences in place of the hedge on the right hand side.

59. The rustic Pump House, steps and bridge in Woodhurst Lane are shown on this postcard which was posted in New Oxted in 1912. Note also the fine beech trees on the right hand side. The scene has not changed very much today except that only the base of the Pump House remains.

2828. Oxted from Rockfield Road.

J.B.Lock's
Real Photo Series.

60. Two comfortable houses and a well-tended garden in Rockfield Road make an interesting foreground to Lock's panoramic view of Oxted, published about 1911. The Oxted Chalk Pit can be seen in the centre of the North Downs and note also the railway sidings to the left and the gas holder in the centre of the photograph.

Barrow Green Road from Chichele Road, Oxted.

61. A steam vehicle can be seen in the centre of this photograph of the northern end of Chichele Road which was posted in 1913. The houses on the left are in Barrow Green Road and the twin gabled house on the right is 44 and 46 Chichele Road. The North Downs are in the background.

Barrow Green Park, Oxted.

Johnson's
Photo Series. 453.

62. Posted from Attwood Cottage, Amy Road, New Oxted in 1919, this postcard shows the mature woodland and miniature waterfalls in Barrow Green Park. The stream rises in the North Downs and continues its journey to Old Oxted, by the Wheatsheaf, and then on to serve the Oxted and Coltsford Mills.

BARROW GREEN COURT,
OXTED. 'ACE' D29

63. Barrow Green Court is featured on an Ace postcard which was posted in 1908. It was the home of the influential Charles Hoskins Master and dates from the early seventeenth century. Today it is a Grade One listed building.

64. Another grand house makes a fine subject for an anonymous postcard publisher. This is Ridgeway House standing proudly in front of the North Downs from a card posted from New Oxted in October 1905.

"Shrubhurst", Oxted. 2

Webster's Photo Series.

65. Shrubhurst, situated close to the railway south of Hurst Green, makes an imposing appearance on this postcard which was published by the Limpsfield company of Webster's about 1912.

Broadham Green, Oxted.

S. & W. Series. 1127.

66. This summer view of Broadham Green was posted in 1921. The nearby Haycutter public house was, in 1892, owned by the local brewery Bushell & Co and the licensee David Longley served the needs of the labouring class.

67. Merle Common County First School has altered but little from this view published by Richardson and posted in 1916. Today there is no evidence of gardening activity but happily the oak tree sill flourishes. The less handsome corrugated iron shed at the rear can also still be seen by the railway line.

St. John's Church, Hurst Green, Oxted. 2264.

H.E.Brockes.

68. St. John the Evangelist's Church is photographed on a Brockes' postcard shortly after it was built in 1912. The church has since undergone an extension to the west (left hand side of photograph). Before 1912 churchgoers would have had to make the journey to St. Mary's, Oxted.

HURST GREEN HALT, OXTED

69. Hurst Green Halt, Oxted is shown here on a postcard published by M. Richardson, Post Office, Holland, Oxted and posted in 1937. The halt was formerly a wooden erection on the south side of the road and was opened on 1st June 1907. Re-sited and built in brick, the modern Hurst Green Station was opened in June 1961.

Hurst Green Halt, Oxted.

Ritchardson's Photo Series.

70. This postcard, posted in 1914, shows the wooden platforms of Hurst Green Halt and its gas lighting. Surrounded by farm land, the railway separates in the distance on its way to Edenbridge (left) and Lingfield and East Grinstead (right).

Knight's Hill, Hurst Green Oxted.

Richardson's Photo Series. 587.

71. Richardson's postcard shows the Hurst Green Road on its way towards Oxted a year or so before the Great War. The furthest houses on the left are Nos. 2 and 4 and the white gable on the right belongs to Laleham Cottages built by pupils and friends in memory of Hannah Pipe in 1900. The photographer was standing on the corner of Mill Lane.

New Holland, Oxted, Surrey.

72. The Hurst Green Road is shown looking away from Oxted in a Homewood postcard posted in 1907. Nunappleton Way has replaced the footpath on the left of the picture and the modern Bromford Close is on the right. The house second from the left was built in 1894.

Holland, Oxted. 2.

Richardsons Photo Series.

73. Looking towards Hurst Green and Oxted, the gabled house on the left is today on the corner of Nunappleton Way which leads to a footbridge over the railway. Holland Lane and the modern Hawthorns are both right hand turnings just outside of the photograph which was posted in 1917.

The Old Cottage, Holland, Oxted

Richardson's
Photo Series. 724.

74. Comfort's Farm Cottage is photographed in 1913 for another Richardson postcard. The ivy has been removed but the cottage is still easily recognisable although there are no longer any timbers visible at the side. The cottage, which stands opposite The Hawthorns, may be older than the eighteenth century date attributed to it.

1734 Holland. Oxted.

75. This charming tiled barn has disappeared from Holland but the single storey building furthest from the camera is easily recognisable as The Diamond public house. Gordon Smith of Stroud Green Road, London, published this postcard about 1906.

Oxted and District Prize Band.

76. The Oxted and District Prize Band proudly displays its trophy and instruments on a post-card published by W. Suter about 1920. Brass bands were a feature of village life locally and postcards exist of other bands at Caterham and Whyteleafe.